Contents

Acknowledgements
Original text by Carl Johnson. Revisions by Graham Knight.
The publishers would like to thank Reebok for their photographic contributions to this book.

All other photographs courtesy of Allsport UK Ltd. Illustrations by Tim Bairstow of Taurus Graphics and Dave Saunders.

Note Throughout the book athletes are referred to individually as 'he'. This should, of course, be taken to mean 'he or she' where appropriate. The performance target table provided for each event represents the rounded average twentieth annual ranking from a major athletics nation. All measurements are in metric units; an imperial conversion is given on page 3.

Introduction

Running is a fundamental activity of Man. In his early history it was essential for his preservation; firstly to enable him to obtain food, and secondly to prevent him from becoming the food of some predator.

The date at which running first became a recreational activity is not recorded, but it is quite certain that it was long before the first documented athletic contests of the ancient Olympic Games in 776 BC. It would have been strange indeed had earlier civilisations, about which there remains scant documentary evidence, not indulged in some form of recreational running. Indeed, the Tailteann Games of Ireland, which contained some running activities, are thought to date back to 1829 BC.

Modern track athletics is an amalgam of several different traditions in pedestrianism: running fast indulges a very basic instinct; endurance running involves separate fundamental elements – in one of its longer forms, it commemorates the legendary feat of the bringing of news of a Greek victory over the Persians at Marathon in 490 BC.

Hurdle racing has distinctly agricultural roots, the original hurdles being the wattle fences used to pen sheep. The first known steeplechase took place over open country near Oxford, England in 1850. It found its way to Oxford University by 1860, and into the modern Olympic programme by 1900 when it was contested at two distances – 2500 m and 4000 m.

The English Cross Country Union dates back to 1883, and the first English Cross Country Championships to 1876.

Walking, as an organised sport, is relatively young. It commenced in England in 1907 and first took its place in the international arena at the 1908 London Olympics.

Conversion table

Metric	Imperial
1 millimetre	0.04 inches
1 centimetre	0.4 inches
1 metre	3.3 feet/
	1.1 yards
1 kilometre	0.62 miles
1 gram	0.03 ounces
1 kilogram	2.2 pounds
1 litre	1.76 pints

Competition

The track

The modern track is elliptical in shape having two parallel 'straights' or 'stretches' joined by two semi-circular bends. It is 400 m around, measured at a distance of 30 cm from the inside edge, or 'kerb'. Depending upon the status of the facility, the track will be divided into six to ten individual lanes, each 1.22–1.25 m wide. A basic plan, with starts and staggers, is shown in fig. 1.

Sprint races (distances up to and including 400 m) are run in these separate lanes throughout. 800 m races use them as far as the end of the first bend (120 m approx.) and the 4 x 400 m relay uses them for one complete lap plus the first bend (500 m approx.).

The start

In all races using lanes and involving a bend, the start is staggered so that the runner in each lane starts ahead of his inner neighbour by a measured amount. This way, no runner loses out to a rival as the result to having to run a greater distance in outer lanes. Lane measurements, other than those for the inside lane, are made 20 cm out from the inner lane line.

Lanes are numbered from inside to outside consecutively, or from left to right in the direction of running on a straight track.

In races above 1500 m (which are not run in lanes), a curved start mark is used.

The finish

All races taking place on a modern running track have a common finish at the end of the 'home straight'. It is marked by a line drawn at right angles to the inside edge of the track where the straight joins the bend. The use of a finishing tape is no longer obligatory.

▼ *Fig. 1 Track layout showing starts and staggers.*
For relay change-over zones see page 15.

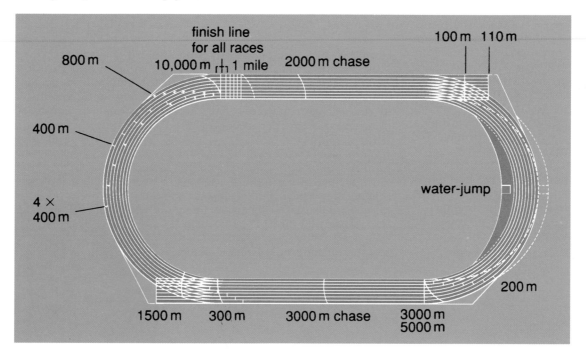

Equipment

The facilities used for track events consist almost entirely of major items which are the property of the stadium owners, and are thus their responsibility. These items include photo-finish equipment, electronic timing displays, stands for judges and timekeepers, lap indicator boards, bells, water-jumps, steeplechase barriers, hurdles and starting blocks.

While athletes and coaches only have a distant interest in photo-finish equipment, they have an acute involvement with hurdles and starting blocks; they may even possess their own versions of the latter.

Hurdles

Hurdles need to be adjustable, from 1.067 m down to 0.762 m, but may well go lower, depending upon national modifications to cater for hurdlers in younger age categories. They are manufactured to strict specifications, with maxima of 1.20 m width, 0.70 m base length and 10 kg total weight. Adjustable counterweights are attached to the base of each so that, whatever the height, it will take a force of at least 3.6 kg to overturn them. Since they have to be adjustable, they need to be kept well greased and require constant careful maintenance.

Starting blocks

Starting blocks are required to be rigid and fasten to the track so as to cause the minimum damage to its surface. Athletes are allowed to use blocks of any design or construction provided that they comply with the above requirements and give no unfair advantage to the user. Owners of synthetic tracks are permitted to insist on their own blocks only being used.

Clothing

Clothing is required to be non-transparent, even when wet, and designed and worn so as not to cause offence.

Footwear, if worn, must not be capable of affording the wearer unfair assistance. Ridges, grooves or other indentations are permitted on both sole and heel provided that they are of the same basic material as the sole. Each shoe may also carry up to 11 spikes. On synthetic surfaces, these may not exceed 9 mm; on non-synthetic surfaces up to 25 mm is allowed. In both instances, the maximum diameter of each spike is set at 4 mm. (There are separate regulations for field athletes.)

Competitors are required to wear identification numbers on their chest and back. Where photo-finish equipment is used, the organisers are empowered to require athletes to wear additional adhesive numbers on the side of their shorts.

▲ *Long-distance*

▲ *Sprint*

7

Preparation

Warm-up is necessary before commencing vigorous activity. Its purpose is to raise the internal temperature of the body and make the tissues surrounding joints more pliable. This facilitates:

• greater range of movement and thereby more effective application of force
• less chance of injury.

Warming up should occupy the first 20 to 40 minutes of training. It should begin with five to ten minutes of gentle exercise such as jogging, on a soft surface such as a grass in-field (in preference to the cinder or synthetic surface of a track).

This gradual beginning should lead into ten to 15 minutes of stretching exercises in which all joint complexes should be progressively exercised to their outer limits of movement. It is important to pay particular attention to those parts of the body that are going to have to work the hardest in the training or competition to follow. It is also important to bear in mind that such a session is an integral part of the warm-up, and in no way suffices for specialised stretching, should that be needed. Such work must be undertaken separately.

The types of exercises that can be suitably incorporated into warm-up stretching are illustrated in fig. 2.

Easing down after competition and training is an equally beneficial activity. Its purpose is to reduce body temperature and pulse rate slowly so that blood flow through the muscles remains relatively high and the waste products resulting from exercise are removed. In this way post-exercise stiffness and soreness are eliminated. It need not take so long as warm-up, nor be so complex; five to 15 minutes of easy jogging, walking and stretching will suffice.

triceps

upper back

8

obliques *groin* *hamstrings* *outer thigh*

chest *quadriceps* *calf* *hip flexors*

The sprints

The 60/100 metres

These events are the speciality of those athletes blessed with blistering speed. Both are run on straight tracks.

The 100 metres is the standard short sprint competition distance and the 60 metres is its indoor equivalent. The race involves a start, followed by a rapid acceleration (or 'pick up') which takes the athlete to between 40 m and 60 m (for the 100 metres event). Beyond 60 m, there is a decrease in speed which the athlete attempts to minimise by relaxing. The final portion of the race is characterised by the 'lift' (designed to maintain leg speed and reduce speed loss) and the finish.

The evolution of starting has taken us to the 'sprint start' for which special starting blocks are used and in which the athlete crouches behind the start line.

International rules make the use of starting blocks and the crouch position mandatory, although some national associations do not adhere to this rigidly for domestic competition. When blocks are used, the athlete's hands must be in contact with the ground when in the 'set' position.

Athletes are eliminated from the competition after two 'false starts' (leaving the blocks before the command), except in combined events competitions, in which one further false start is permitted before exclusion.

The basic form of the crouch start is generally referred to as the 'medium' start:

- the front foot is placed 35-45 cm behind the start line
- the rear foot is placed 35-45 cm behind the front foot

- in the set position, the angle behind the front knee should be 90 degrees
- in the set position, the rear leg should be slightly flexed
- the rear block face should be set at a steeper angle than the front one.

The most common modification to the medium start is moving the feet closer together and slightly further back from the start line. Such changes are essentially matters of personal preference and comfort in the set position.

Starting tips

- Raise your hips to just above shoulder height on the command 'Set'.
- Do not let your shoulders move in advance of your hands and let your weight act mainly through your front foot.
- Move gradually into the erect position as you run out from the blocks.

The starting commands for all races up to and including the 400 metres are: 'On your marks', 'Set' (or their equivalent in the starter's own language), then when all are steady in the set position, the gun is fired.

During the pick-up phase, in which great acceleration takes place, work hard against the ground in the initial stages, changing to lighter, more agile movements as top speed is reached. Speed is maintained by running 'tall' (keeping the hips and chest high) with a high knee-lift and 'clawing' foot contacts (pulling the foot backwards) which pull the athlete along each time the foot strikes the ground.

Towards the end of the race, the lift is achieved by making the running action lighter and quicker. The 'dip' finish, in which the athlete thrusts his torso forwards at the line, is often mistimed: it loses its value if begun before the final stride to the line.

Performance targets (in seconds) – 100 metres

	Adults	U-20	U-17	U-15
Male	10.40	10.75	11.00	11.50
Female	11.80	12.10	12.30	12.50

The 200 metres

200 metre sprinters, while as quick as their 100 metre counterparts, must also be capable of maintaining high speeds over longer distances, and of mastering the special skill of running the bend.

The 200 metres race begins at the bend diagonally opposite the finish line. The starts are staggered so that the distance to the finish is the same for each competitor. On a standard track, lane 2's start line is 3.51 m in advance of that of lane 1, and subsequent start lines are 3.83 m in advance of each inside adjacent one.

The fact that the start takes place on a curve establishes two starting principles in addition to those of the 100 metre start:

• the starting blocks are positioned to the outside of the lane, facing at a tangent to the visible crown of the left-hand lane line
• the left hand is placed some 5 cm behind the start line to prevent the shoulder axis from being skewed in relation to the spine's axis.

The pick-up should not be quite so forceful as that for the 100 metres, the race being run with more control and conservation of energy. The first 100 m should be run in 0.2 to 0.4 seconds slower than the sprinter's best 100 metres. Around the curve, the athlete will need to lean slightly inwards and press the left shoulder forwards a little in order to counteract centripetal forces and increase efficiency.

The most difficult part of the race occurs where the bend joins the straight. Top speed has been reached and the accumulated centripetal forces of the bend are at their greatest. Continuation of the bend techniques, coupled with relaxed, light, high cadence running will resolve the difficulties adequately.

Speed decrements towards the end of the race are greater in 200 metre running than in the 100 metres. The 200 metre specialist must thus undertake a slightly heavier training load, over longer distances (200/300/400 m) in order to reduce these to a minimum.

Although it is advantageous to run close to the left-hand lane line (except in the inner lanes of a track having very tight bends), it must not be forgotten that to run on or beyond that line risks disqualification.

Performance targets (in seconds) – 200 metres

	Adults	U-20	U-17	U-15
Male	21.20	22.00	22.50	23.50
Female	24.10	24.90	25.30	26.00

The 400 metres

The 400 metre race represents sprinting at the limit of a sprinter's lactic anaerobic energy supply system. It lasts for one complete lap of the 400 metre track.

The event begins at the finish line, and because two bends are used, the staggered starts necessary from lane 2 outwards are quite considerable – 7.04 m in advance of lane 1, and then 7.67 m in advance of the adjacent inside lane thereafter.

The successful completion of the race is reliant on the realisation of a planned economical energy expenditure in which speed is combined with the ability to withstand intense effort – in other words, the development of a resistance to lactic acid build-up. The resultant 400 metre time should approximate to twice the sprinter's best 200 metre time, plus 3 or 4 seconds.

The pick-up phase will not be as accentuated as that of the 100 metres, or even the 200 metres. Full speed need not be attained until the second 100 m has been entered. The middle of the race should be given over to running at the target pace with a long, controlled stride. This pace should be sustained into the second bend but more effort will be needed to maintain it as the bend unwinds. Should the first half of the race be run too fast, this final phase may leave the sprinter struggling.

Whatever way the first 300 m has been run, the last 80 m will represent an effort to maintain a controlled stride against the 'tying up' effect of increasing fatigue.

A large proportion of 400 metre training is designed to stimulate and develop the activity of the lactic anaerobic energy supply system and to make the athlete oblivious to the unpleasant effects of lactate build-up.

The 400 metre sprinter takes the same risks as the 200 metre specialist in having to run close to the left-hand lane line without crossing or stepping on it.

Performance targets (in seconds) – 400 metres

	Adults	U-20	U-17	U-15
Male	47.10	48.80	50.50	53.50
Female	54.50	57.00	(Female U-17 athletes are not encouraged to run 400 m in competition)	

The relays

The 4 x 100 metres

The 4 x 100 metres relay involves four sprinters combining forces to move a 50 g circular hollow tube, called a 'baton', around one lap of the track. The baton is 28–30 cm in length and 12–13 cm in circumference.

It is passed from one sprinter to another within a 20 m long change-over zone straddling each 100 m section of the race; these zones are marked with yellow lines on synthetic tracks by international convention. Each change-over zone is preceded by a 10 m long acceleration (or pre-change-over) zone, marked by an orange line and within which the outgoing runner can stand. However, the baton must not be exchanged in this area.

The baton is thus carried for 106 m, 100 m, 100 m and 94 m by each successive carrier, assuming that it is exchanged in the front third of the

change-over zone when the speed of the outgoing runner is at its highest. Each thus runs 106 m, 126 m, 126 m and 120 m, since they run alongside each other for part of the time through the change-over zone.

Because 'legs' 1 and 3 involve running a bend, common sense dictates that those runners run close to the left-hand lane line, in the same way that 200 metre runners do, and enter the acceleration and change-over zones on that course. It therefore follows that outgoing runners 2 and 4 must stand and run in a line which takes them on the right-hand side of their lane, so that a collision is avoided when the incoming runner comes alongside. It also follows that the incoming runner must carry the baton in his right hand and the outgoing runner receive it in the left.

Having started to the right of their lane, runners 2 and 4, who run the straights, can remain where they are

without affecting the smoothness and efficiency of the run. Runner 2 is the only one of this pair who has to 'give' the baton, and being on the right of the lane enables runner 3 to start to the left of the lane, receive in his right hand and continue on that line of running.

The baton is passed using either a 'down-pass' or an 'up-pass'. Properly executed, the down-pass has the potential to be the quicker since it permits about a metre of 'free distance' between each athlete. The up-pass is safer because it is still easier to put together a change even if the incoming runner gets ahead of his outgoing partner. Such a compromise is almost impossible using the down-pass method.

One disadvantage of the up-pass is that it requires runner 1 to grasp the first quarter of the baton; runner 2 then takes hold of the second quarter, runner 3 the third quarter, and runner 4 the final quarter. Because the baton is only 30 cm long, the technique demands that each passer gets close enough to the receiver to be able to press the back of his hand against the palm of the receiver's hand as the exchange is made. Failure to do so will result in the receiver taking hold of the wrong quarter, runner 3 having no baton to give to runner 4, and thus having to make emergency adjustments to his hold on the baton as he is running in order to effect a compromise change. Batons are often dropped in such circumstances.

Runners must practise changes and work out 'check marks'. These are placed on the track at a point in front of where the incoming runner reaches the beginning of the acceleration zone, and enable the outgoing runner to start as his partner passes the mark, run flat out and yet be caught by the incoming runner in the final third of the change-over zone. This mark will be approximately 5.5 m from the beginning of the acceleration zone for inexperienced athletes, and 7.3–7.9 m for club runners; it is positioned at the side of the lane along which the incoming runner is travelling.

Key points

- The incoming runner continues running flat out until after the baton has been passed on.
- The incoming runner calls 'Hand' or 'Stick' when close enough to exchange the baton.
- The outgoing runner presents a steady hand on the call and waits until he feels the baton in his hand.
- The incoming runner places the baton firmly into the receiver's hand.

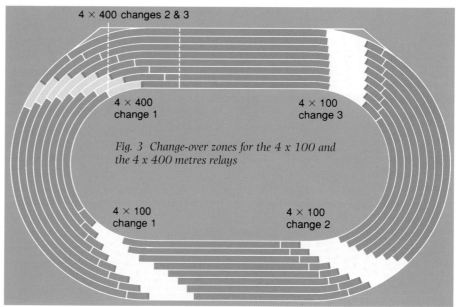

Fig. 3 Change-over zones for the 4 x 100 and the 4 x 400 metres relays

15

The 4 x 400 metres

This race involves four runners combining to move the baton around four laps of the track, each running one lap in the process.

The first 500 m of the race is run in lanes; thus the starts are staggered even more than those for the 400 metres, and the first change-over is in advance of that for subsequent ones. (The method of calculating and measuring them is fully explained in the handbook of the International Amateur Athletic Federation (IAAF).) There is no acceleration zone. The international colour code for the change-overs is blue, and the start lines have a blue bar at their centre.

The point at which runner 2 is permitted to leave his lane and cut to the track kerb is identical to that used by 800 metre runners and is marked by a green line across the lanes.

Since the incoming runner is very fatigued, the exchange must be visual (unlike that of the 4 x 100 metres), with the outgoing runner assuming the greater responsibility for a successful transfer. He judges when to start running and takes the baton in his left hand as he moves away from the zone. This permits the incoming runner to remain on the left-hand side of the lane, the outgoing runner occupying the right-hand side, and provides some shield against collisions with other runners. The baton must thus be presented from the right of the incoming athlete, and must therefore be exchanged from left to right hand at some time during the run. The best time to do this is immediately after clearing the change-over zone.

Runners 3 and 4 take up their positions at the beginning of the change-over zone according to the position in which their incoming runner is lying, i.e. second from the kerb if lying second, third if lying third, etc. This is straightforward when positions are clearly defined but, in practice, last-minute changes of running position frequently occur. As a result, the change-overs can become quite combative.

17

Hurdling

The 100/110 metres hurdles

In the shorter of the two sprint hurdles events, adult men race over 110 m and women over 100 m in order to accommodate the different average statures of the sexes. The differences in the races are set out in the table at the bottom of this page. In some parts of the world, adjustments are made to racing distances and the numbers of barriers covered in order to accommodate younger athletes.

The base of the hurdle has to be weighted so that it takes a force of at least 3.6 kg to knock it over.

It must never be forgotten that the sprint hurdles is a speed event, and that a good hurdler will have to train often as a sprinter. That said, many elements of the event are a compromise for a sprinter:

- at the start, the feet may have to be placed in the least preferred position in order to reach the take-off ideally positioned to hurdle the first barrier
- during the pick-up phase, the athlete has only seven or eight strides in order to come upright
- there is a barrier clearance every fourth stride
- the athlete must prepare for the next clearance between barriers.

On the other hand, certain elements of sprinting have to be exaggerated:

- run 'tall' so that the barrier can be attacked better
- incline forwards in order to aid dynamism across each barrier
- be 'active' coming off the barrier
- maintain high hips through the landing
- concentrate on quick arm actions between barriers: quick arms promote quick legs and fast running.

	Number of hurdles	Hurdle height	Start to hurdle	Distance between	Last hurdle to finish
Men	10	106.7 cm	13.72 m	9.14 m	14.02 m
Women	10	84.0 cm	13.00 m	8.50 m	10.50 m

Performance targets (in seconds) – 100/110 metres hurdles

	Adults	U-20	U-17	U-15
Male	14.50	15.60	(Race specifications differ	
Female	14.10	15.00	from country to country)	

The 400 metres hurdles

In this event, men and women run one circuit of the track, in lanes, hurdling barriers of 91.4 cm and 76.2 cm in height respectively. The first hurdle is spaced 45 m from the start and subsequent hurdles at 35m intervals.

Since the event starts on a bend, the technicalities of the 200 metre and 400 metre start apply. According to the ability of the athlete, it will take between 20 and 24 strides to the first take-off. Thereafter, natural stride length determines the stride pattern between the first few barriers.

A rough correlation exists between the number of strides taken to the first barrier and those subsequently. Thus, a 20 stride approach leads to 13 or 14 between hurdles, 21 to 14 or 15, 22 to 15 or 16, 23 to 16 or 17 and 24 to 17 or 18.

The use of an even number of strides over the early barriers is rare since it requires the ability to hurdle equally well off either leg, and most hurdlers have a preference for one leg

or the other. In a competitive situation, it is more secure to lead with the left leg, since leading with the right can cause disqualification through trailing the inner leg around the barrier. This is a particular problem as the runner keeps close to the left-hand side of the lane when negotiating the bend.

At hurdles 5 or 6, the onset of fatigue will bring about an increase in the number of strides between barriers. Whether this progresses through one additional stride for two barriers, then to two strides more, will depend on the athlete's ability to hurdle from the 'wrong' leg. The more gradual the change, the better it is likely to be.

Performance targets (in seconds) – 400 metres hurdles

	Adults	U-20	U-17	U-15
Male	52.00	55.30	(Race specifications differ	
Female	60.20	64.50	from country to country)	

▼ *Fig. 4 Sequence of a hurdles clearance, showing the key elements of keeping the hips high while driving at the hurdle, and running 'off' it. Women's body position is more upright then men's.*

Track distance events

The 800 metres

The 800 metres race embraces two complete laps of the track. It is run in lanes as far as the end of the first bend. The starts are thus staggered by approximately the same amount as for the 200 metres, although the actual formula for calculating and measuring the distance is more complicated than this (see the aforementioned IAAF Handbook). Start lines are identified by a green centre bar, according to the IAAF international code of track marking.

The starting command of this event and for all distances above is: 'On your marks' (or its equivalent in the starter's own language) then, when all are steady, the gun is fired. There is no 'Set' command.

The 'break line' (the point at which the athletes are permitted to leave their lanes) is at the junction of the first bend and the back straight and is coloured green; it is the same as that used for the 4 x 400 metres relay. Once past it, athletes may run as close to the track kerb as they wish.

A planned, even utilisation of energy and distribution of effort is appropriate to the running of this event. Conversely, tactics may demand that it is run at a fast pace in order to 'burn off' known 'kickers' (athletes with a sprint finish), or at a more conservative pace in order to permit oneself to 'kick' at the finish.

The event taxes the aerobic/anaerobic energy systems in the ratio of approximately 65:35. Training should reflect this fact.

Training aims

● The development of a well balanced running posture and a springy running action.
● To build up aerobic endurance and work capacity.
● To train the anaerobic energy system in order to develop and combine endurance and speed.
● To develop power (especially in the legs) and general strength endurance.

Performance targets (in minutes/seconds) – 800 metres

	Adults	U-20	U-17	U-15
Male	1:48.5	1:52.5	1:57.5	2:05.0
Female	2:06.0	2:12.0	2:15.0	2:18.0

The 1500 metres

The 1500 metres event, also known as the 'metric mile', is run over three-and-three-quarter laps of the track. The start is made from a specially constructed white line which curves across the lanes just before the end of the first bend.

The athletes line up in race order, but not necessarily with each occupying a lane. As soon as the gun goes they may cut across to the track kerb provided that they do not jostle or obstruct another competitor so as to impede his progress in the process.

Running to a planned energy utilisation and effort distribution is as important as it is to the 800 metres event, perhaps even more so. Running next to the kerb helps to achieve this, provided that the athlete does not let himself become 'boxed in' by other competitors so that it is not possible to get out when necessary. To run wider than the outside of the second lane, particularly around bends, increases the distance and is unnecessarily wasteful of energy.

The balance between the aerobic/anaerobic energy systems is in a ratio of approximately 50:50. Thus, compared to the 800 metres event, an even better aerobic base has to be developed, combined with a strong need for simultaneous aerobic/anaerobic power through the LAO_2 energy system.

The development of a sound, efficient running technique is as valid for this event as it is for those shorter and faster ones.

Performance targets (in minutes/seconds) – 1500 metres

	Adults	U-20	U-17	U-15
Male	3:42.0	3:53.0	4:04.0	4:18.0
Female	4:20.0	4:36.0	4:40.0	4:48.0

23

The steeplechase

This is currently a championship event for men only, although after the 2000 Sydney Olympic Games there will be steeplechase events for women at all major championships. The men's event is run over 3000 m, the women's over 2000 m, with respective barrier heights of 91.4 cm (men) and 76.2 cm (women).

The race takes place over seven laps plus part of a lap (for the 3000 m event) or five laps plus part of a lap (2000 m). The laps may be 390 m or 410 m long, depending on whether the water-jump is positioned inside or outside the second bend; the former is more common. The four barriers plus the water-jump are 79 m or 82 m apart and the 3000 m start is positioned either half-way down the back straight or two-thirds of the way around the second bend. The 2000 metre start is positioned halfway down the home straight. It is not possible to run the shorter event with an outside water-jump. In both races, the first barrier is not introduced until over 200 m have been run and the water-jump is not introduced until after the first portable barrier has been crossed.

All barriers are solid enough for the athlete to be able to jump on and off with safety.

The event demands the abilities of a fast middle-distance runner coupled with sufficient competence and agility to cross the barriers. At club level, technical ability need not be great, but to compete well the steeplechaser needs to be a competent hurdler and also a proficient water-jumper. Since it takes about 0.4 seconds to cross a hurdle and 1 second to cross the water-jump (and one can easily lose between 0.1 and 0.2 seconds crossing each), a total of 1 second can be gained or lost per lap. The ability to hurdle from either leg is thus a useful bonus.

The water-jump calls for a special technique which involves stepping on to the barrier, then pushing hard with the supporting leg to project oneself over the water; this way, the landing is made far enough into the water, on the other leg, so that one can step out on the subsequent stride. It pays to keep the hips low and the supporting leg bent while on the barrier rail. It also helps to delay the push off until the body weight has passed beyond the rail, and then to push back against the rail in order to maximise the drive.

The steeplechaser also needs to be effective between barriers and must train mid-range endurance abilities.

The proficient steeplechaser will need to dedicate training time to hurdling. Moreover, he will need to learn to hurdle from both legs in the manner of a 400 metre hurdler so that he can accommodate the barrier without any restriction, however it is presented to him. This ability is very important since the barrier has often to be sighted through a crowd of other runners, who make it difficult to judge distances and to adjust stride patterns in the approach.

▼ *Fig. 5 The steeplechaser stays low as he steps on to the water-jump barrier, and drives out from it so that he steps just into the water near its far edge.*

Performance targets (in minutes/seconds) – steeplechase

	Adults	U-20	U-17	U-15
Male (3000 m)	8:50.0	—	—	—
Female (2000 m)	—	—	—	—

The 5000 metres

The 5000 metres is the shorter of the two long distance events run at major championships by both men and women.

The race starts from a curved white line situated at the beginning of the second bend, identical to the 3000 metre start. It is run over a distance of 12½ laps.

Its aerobic/anaerobic requirement is in a ratio of roughly 80:20. There is also a greater likelihood that mid-race speed surges will be necessary, or will have to be countered. Endurance speed, incorporating change of pace, is thus a prerequisite.

It follows that resistance to lactic acid build-up is also important. It can be achieved in training by seeking protracted efforts of longer than 40 seconds, made at faster than racing speed and with short breaks of 2 to 4 minutes. The total suggested distance of such sessions is between 3 km and 4 km.

The 10,000 metres

The 10,000 metres, also known as the '10 k', is the longer of the two long distance endurance events run at major championships. It is contested by women as well as men.

It commences at the start/finish point, from a curved white start line, and progresses through 25 laps of the track.

The race's aerobic/anaerobic ratio requirement is approximately 85:15. Although the training is very similar to that of the 5000 metres, running for over 30 minutes requires an extension of endurance capacity. Due to this fact, racing ought to be sparse and for mature runners only. Oxygen consumption during the race is in the region of 180 litres, and this suggests that the quantity of training should increase by some 30%, the bulk of which should be of a continuous fast nature.

Performance targets (in minutes/seconds) – 5000 metres

	Adults	U-20	U-17	U-15
Male	13:50.0	15:30.0	—	—
Female	16:30.0	—	—	—

Performance targets (in minutes/seconds) – 10,000 metres

	Adults	U-20	U-17	U-15
Male	29:10.0	—	—	—
Female	35:30.0	—	—	—

Non-track distance events

Cross-country running

Cross-country races are endurance competitions run over open countryside. A limited area of ploughed land may be included, but the traversing of roads should be kept to a minimum. This form of racing lends itself to commons, heathland, parkland or race courses.

Obstacles are intended to be included in the course since they are an integral part of the natural countryside, but they should not be so severe that they elevate in importance other abilities above that of running. The use of artificial obstacles is frowned upon. For reasons of safety, obstacles – together with the course flags or posts – should be clearly visible from a distance of 125 m. Equally, competitors must be permitted an unhampered run – with no constrictions – for the first 1500 m of the race.

Internationally accepted racing distances are 12 km for senior men, 6 km for senior women, 8 km for Under-20 men and 4 km for Under-20 women. For younger age groups, national associations modify races according to their own particular needs. Contact your national organisation for details.

Cross-country races are usually organised as team competitions over and above the individual competition. Teams will consist of several runners. Each finisher is assigned a placement score. A placement total for a pre-arranged proportion of each team is made and positions are allocated on the basis of the lowest team scores. These races provide an enjoyable interlude to the winter grind of stamina building for the endurance fraternity, many of whom even make the activity their main interest in preference to competing during the summer track season.

The race is started in the standard fashion for an endurance event. In instances when large numbers of competitors take part, they are lined up in team files and a 5 minute warning is given, with intermediate warnings if deemed necessary.

Unlike road racing, refreshments are not permitted during the race, even though the senior men's event is beyond 10 km.

The finish is best organised as a funnel so that competitors are herded into a single file beyond the finishing line in order that finishing positions can be allocated efficiently. A multiple funnel may be necessary when very large fields are involved.

Cross-country tactics over and above those of endurance track races mainly consist of exerting pressure on opponents at times in the race when the tendency is to switch off slightly, both mentally and physically. Such opportunities generally present themselves on the crests of hills, at the ends of fast downhill sections of the course, after sharp turns or when emerging from restricted sections or over obstacles.

Road racing

The 1970s witnessed a boom in road running activity, fed by a general increase in health consciousness and exercise, which gathered much of its momentum in the US. This boom generated such worldwide interest and participation in jogging, fun-running and road racing that these areas now make up the most active sector of the sport.

The marathon (see page 33) holds pride of place among road races and is perhaps the most well known and best understood. However, internationally recognised distances range from 15 km to 30 km (at 5 km intervals) and there are also the half marathon (21 km) and many other races staged at all sorts of distances – even as short as 1½km.

Some races, such as the London to Brighton (86 km) and the Comrades Marathon from Durban to Pietermaritzburg (87 km), are generally referred to as 'ultra-distance' races and occupy an important niche in the world calendar of road running. In ultra-running events, road and track become entwined and best performances are recognised separately under both conditions at regular intervals up to 1600 km or six days.

The measurement of courses is strictly standardised. In events of more than 10 km, sponging and drinking stations must be provided at regular intervals; at distances over 20 km, feeding or refreshment stations must be provided every 5 km, with sponging and drinking stations midway between each.

Great care is taken to oversee the safety of competitors during these races and to prevent them from pushing themselves to such an extent that they endanger themselves in the process.

The aerobic/anaerobic balance for 10 km road running is the same as that for the 10,000 metres race on the track (*see* page 28). In marathon running, the ratio is roughly 98:2. Training will need to range in nature from that required for 10,000 metre running to that being totally composed of extensive continuous running, aggregating around 160 km per week and including some runs of 30 km duration – this represents the requirements of races over marathon-type distances.

In the longer races, the athlete is attempting to run at the outer limits of energy supply and so pre-race and intra-race dietary care is prudent. For example, ensure that the available energy value of the pre-prepared drinks that you take meets your particular needs; it is equally important to arrange for someone to actually hand your drinks to you at each station.

Since courses vary greatly – some flat, others hilly – performance targets are specific to each race. The following approximations are offered.

Age	20–39	40–49	50+	Women
10 miles	53 mins	63 mins	70 mins	73 mins
20 km	68 mins	80 mins	89 mins	92 mins
½ marathon	71 mins	86 mins	94 mins	100 mins
25 km	76 mins	104 mins	115 mins	120 mins
20 miles	114 mins	140 mins	230 mins	—
100 km	470 mins	470 mins	—	590 mins
24 hrs	200 km	200 km	—	180 km

The marathon

The marathon is perhaps the original road race, that from which all others evolved. Yet since the beginning of the modern Olympic Games, it has taken up a legitimate residence within the realm of the sport of track and field because of its uniqueness as a necessary inclusion in all major games and as a symbol of the Olympic ethos. It begins and ends in the competitive stadium.

The challenge of 'beating the distance' is possibly greater than that of winning, or of beating rivals. Merely completing the race is a huge initial motivation, and this has accorded the marathon enormous popularity in the world of road running.

Until 1908, marathon courses were approximately 40 km in length. At the Games of that year the course was lengthened to 26 miles 385 yds (42 km) in order that it could start on the Royal lawns of Windsor castle and finish in front of the Royal box at the stadium. It has remained so ever since. Refreshment and sponging stations need to be provided in accordance with the rules governing races of more than 20 km (*see* page 31).

Since the race is conducted at the upper limits of the aerobic energy supply, training will reflect this fact and be composed almost exclusively of continuous extensive running, including at least one run per week of 30 km, and totalling some 160 km per week. One 'Fartlek' session (*see* page 37) or a fast continuous run per week will prepare the athlete for the small anaerobic requirements of the event.

At about 32–34 km into the race, the body's 'easy' energy supply (i.e. that deriving from glycogen) becomes exhausted and a change to less accessible fat stores takes place. This is accompanied by a rapid deterioration in both pace and in the capacity to keep going. It is known colloquially as 'hitting the wall'. The practice of using a special diet during the week preceding the race in order to boost glycogen stores artificially and thereby postpone this depletion during the race, became very popular during the 1970s. However, a more circumspect attitude has taken over because of associated side effects. e.g. the discovery of unpleasant lassitude experienced during the three-day carbohydrate abstinence which follows the long glycogen 'bleed-out' run of the first day and during which training must continue, albeit at a reduced level.

A novice potential marathon runner should average at least 15 km per day, or 100 km per week, for 24 weeks in order to have any chance of completing the course.

Performance targets (in hours/minutes) – marathon

	Adults	U-20	U-17	U-15
Male	2:20	—	—	—
Female	2:45	—	—	—

Walking

Walking is defined as *progression by steps so taken that unbroken contact with the ground is maintained. At each step, the advancing foot of the walker must make contact with the ground before the rear foot leaves the ground.*

Races take place over 20 km for men and women, and over 50 km for men at most major international events. They are usually started inside the stadium, and then the athletes cover most of the distance on the roads outside before returning to the stadium for the finish. Non-championship competitions take place on both road and track over a variety of distances ranging from 2 km to 160 km or even 24 hours.

In one sense, walking is an endurance event, often a long one – 50 km is further than the marathon. But it demands a high technical content too, representing a critical part in successful performance at all levels.

Although race walking is a derivative of ordinary walking, it has been modified considerably to enable athletes to walk at speeds approaching 15 km per hour. These changes evolved as the event became an athletic discipline and the resulting technique is the natural way to walk at such speeds.

The most significant modification is that, at speed, the pelvis rotates horizontally about the spine with the hip-joint moving ahead of the spine on each stride. Longer strides are thus possible. This action is coupled to a declination of the pelvis above the swinging leg as it shifts laterally. The supporting leg flexes as the foot flattens against the ground, as does the swinging leg, in order to move forwards. These actions, coupled to active use of the supporting ankle, smooth out the path of the body's centre of gravity and conserve energy.

Training is not unlike that of the marathon runner. A typical programme might consist of:

- 20–25 km at 50% effort on Saturdays, followed by 20–25 km at 75% effort on Sundays
- 15 km at 75% effort or 10 km at 95% effort on Mondays and Fridays (unless racing)
- 6 x 800 m or 1 km intervals (400 m/600 m rest) Tuesdays
- alternating 50% or 75% effort on Wednesdays.

Performance targets (in minutes/seconds) – walking

	3 km	5 km	10 km	20 km	50 km
Male	12:50	26:00	46:30	96:00	300:00
Female	15:20	27:00	58:30	130:00	360:00

Training

Organisation

An outline plan of annual training is worked back from the date of the anticipated competitive climax, e.g. regional or national championships. For a serious athlete of some years' experience, the starting point will be around 12 months ahead of this date. Separate schematic outlines of such annual programmes are given on pages 38–9. For a complete beginner, the minimum time necessary to attain a reasonable standard of fitness for a first competition is something in the region of 24 weeks.

It is usual to divide the annual build-up into three distinct blocks of training, often referred to as 'macrocycles', which have recuperation, preparation and adjustment, and competition as their successive individual aims.

Recuperation macrocycle

This should be spent as a period of *active* recovery from the training and competition stresses of the previous year, and in evaluation of the past year and planning for the year to come.

Preparation macrocycle

Lasting until the beginning of the next competitive season – some six months – the 'preparation macrocycle' is subdivided into two phases or 'mesocycles'. The first of these (the 'general mesocycle') is devoted to the gradual improvement of the aerobic base, general strength, local muscular endurance, and mobility and technical development, or technical alteration if needed.

This is followed by the 'special mesocycle' which turns towards the specific needs of competing in a particular event. During its earliest weeks, the cycle concentrates on the heightening of the levels of speed/anaerobic/strength endurance and absolute strength (where necessary), coupled with continued technical development. It changes as it progresses to emphasise speed, speed endurance and elastic strength, while continuing strength endurance and technical development during its final weeks.

Competition macrocycle

The 'competition macrocycle' is characterised by a general reduction in training quantity, though not quality, in order to maximise energy and focus on the achievement of competitive goals. For those in the shorter running events, in which a number of peaks are possible during the season, it may be prudent to return to a period of hard training during the mid-cycle phase so as to be able to attain higher levels of performance during the final weeks, or even just to maintain form.

This is not possible in those longer events in which recovery times between peaks of effort can be more extended.

It must not be overlooked that recovery is just as important an element of training as work. It is all too easy to become hooked on increasing the work rate to such an extent that time fails to be assigned to regeneration; such is a recipe for disaster. A hard day followed by an easier day; no more than three working days in succession; two recovery days in every fortnight; one easy week in every month – these provide the usual ways of ensuring that an athlete is not excessively worked, and must be included in the overall training plan.

Systems

Training attempts to improve the systems of energy supply for activity. Its two mechanisms are:

• the immediate short-term energy supply, or *anaerobic* mechanism. It has two sub-divisions: the *alactic anaerobic* is very short lived (no longer than about 10 secs) and produces no lactate as a by-product; the *lactic anaerobic* extends the process up to about 40 secs and produces carbon dioxide, water and lactic acid as by-products
• the long-term energy supply – the aerobic (or O_2) mechanism – which, unlike its counterpart, requires oxygen in order to operate.

There are three main systems for running and walking training.

(1) **Continuous**, in which a run of a single duration is completed at a fixed pace. It has two sub-divisions:

• steady runs of medium pace carried out close to the anaerobic threshold (the point at which significant levels of lactate begin to accumulate) over distances of 4 km to 10 km. Threshold pulse rates can be established in the physiology laboratory but cannot be estimated easily, although a rough-and-ready index occurs when one ceases to be able to converse easily while running
• steady runs of slow pace but long duration (30 minutes or more), conducted at pulse rates between the anaerobic threshold and its aerobic equivalent, which can be calculated using the formula $70\% \times ([220 - age] - resting\ pulse) + resting\ pulse$. These runs provide the main endurance base for the longer events in particular.

The aerobic effect of this type of training is long term.

(2) **Intermittent**, in which several runs alternate with periods of rest. The rests may be either active or passive. There are two types:

• interval training, which develops the aerobic side of endurance, and which itself is further divided into:

(i) short intervals of between 200 m and 400 m in length with rests of between 30 seconds and 3 minutes, or (ii) long intervals of over 800 m, with recovery periods of between 1 and 5 minutes.

The aerobic effect of this type of training tends to be short term.

• repetition training, which works on the anaerobic side of endurance, and which has three sub-divisions:

(i) speed training, conducted over very short distances in order to develop sheer speed. Recoveries here need to be somewhere in the region of 4 to 6 minutes

(ii) short distance/short recovery training over distances up to 400 m, in which the recovery time should roughly equal that of the run. It, in turn, can be separated into:

– strength endurance, in which quality is sacrificed by keeping rigidly to recovery times so that the session rapidly hurts

– speed endurance, in which individual runs are grouped in sets, with a longer recovery span between each set, in order to maintain quality over more runs

(iii) long duration/long recovery training over distances from 300 m to 1000 m, in which recovery may last up to 10 minutes in order to keep work output at its highest. Speed runners will work over shorter distances than endurance runners.

Speed is the essence of this work. Runs need to be made at greater than 80% of the best performance for the distance.

(3) Mixed pace training or 'Fartlek', in which changes of pace are incorporated into a continuous run. These pace surges may be pre-planned and controlled, or allowed to evolve naturally depending on how the athlete feels.

'Paarlauf' running is a form of mixed pace training involving two athletes operating a continuous relay on a track. 'Legs' may be 200 m or 300 m long, and recovery jogs roughly 100 m. It is also possible to use the arrangement in groups of three for short interval work – this is particularly suitable for beginners.

Sample annual programme: speed runners

	Sept	Oct	Nov	Dec	Jan	Feb	Mar	Apr	May	Jun	Jul	Aug
Macrocycles	Rest	PREPARATION							COMPETITION			
Mesocycles	Rest	Phase 1				Phase 2			Phase 1	Phase 2	Phase 3	
STRENGTH TRAINING		Foundation phase				Strength gain	Power develop		Strength retention	Return to PREPARATION Phase 2		Strength retention
Type		Callisthenic or multigym circuits Free weights				Multigym but mainly free weights			Free weights			Free weights
Loading		50-80% (of maximum)				85-100%	75-85%		90%			90%
Frequency		× 2-3 (per week)					× 2-3		× 1			× 1
ELASTIC STRENGTH (special training)		Endurance bounding				Depth jumps Plyometrics	Very short fast runs from blocks		Competitive running			Competitive running
RUNNING TRAINING		Mainly aerobic Duration runs Medium repetitions Some speed endurance				Anaerobic Hill runs Speed endurance Some speed	Short reps Accent on speed Occasional medium reps		Occasional medium reps Short fast reps Accent on speed			Occasional medium reps Short fast reps Accent on speed
SKILL TRAINING		× 1 unless relearning is needed				cont.	More often × 2-3		× 1-2 depending on competition programme			
MOBILITY TRAINING		Daily throughout the training year										

Sample annual programme: endurance runners

	Sept	Oct	Nov	Dec	Jan	Feb	Mar	Apr	May	Jun	Jul	Aug
Macrocycles	Rest	PREPARATION							COMPETITION			
Mesocycles	Rest	Phase 1				Phase 2			Phase 1	Phase 2		Phase 3
STRENGTH TRAINING		Foundation phase				Strength gain	Power develop		Strength retention	Return to PREPARATION Phase 2		Strength retention
Type		Callisthenic or multigym circuits				Mainly multigym but some free weights			Free weights			Free weights
Loading		50–70% (of maximum)				70–85%	85%+		90%			90%
Frequency		× 2–3 (per week)				× 2–3			× 1			× 1
ELASTIC STRENGTH (special training)		Endurance bounding				Depth jumps Plyometrics			Competitive running			Competitive running
RUNNING TRAINING		Mainly aerobic Duration runs Long repetitions				Aerobic & anaerobic Hill runs Shorter & faster	Shorter reps Race pace runs Accent on speed		Occasional medium reps Short fast reps Accent on speed			Occasional medium reps Short fast reps Accent on speed
SKILL TRAINING		× 1 unless relearning is needed				cont.	More often × 2–3		× 1–2 depending on competition programme			
MOBILITY TRAINING		Daily throughout the training year										

Weekly cycle

What an athlete does on each day of the week is determined by lifestyle and access to facilities. Each week thus becomes a cyclic entity – a 'microcycle'.

Taking account of the fact that it is best to progress through days devoted firstly to preparation, followed by adaptation, then to application, and that some time needs to be allocated to recovery, the athlete arrives at a four-day cycle of three days of increasing intensity, followed by one day of recuperation. Within such a structure the principle of 'hard day, easy day', related to the distance run, should be applied. The seven day week, however, forces compromise.

A further compromise is forced by popular winter cross-country or road racing programmes which encourage loss of focus and an inability to perform well during the winter or the summer. It is very important to decide whether the aim is to do well as a cross-country or road runner, or as a track athlete. Having made the decision, maintain a clear focus. The following table provides examples of resulting weekly organisation.

	Standard			
	Young novice club athlete	Young club athlete beyond novice	Adult club athlete	Week preceding competition
Monday	—	—	Road/ country running	Longest running
Tuesday	Training	Repetition & conditioning	Repetition & conditioning	Repetition & conditioning
Wednesday	—	Road/ country running	Road/ country running	Medium road/ country running
Thursday	Training	Repetition & conditioning	Repetition & conditioning	Short fast running
Friday	—	—	Road/ country running	—
Saturday	—	Road/ country running	—	Competition
Sunday	Training	Longest running	Longest running	Recovery running
Comments	Club sessions	Need for extra conditioning recognised and accommodated	Conditioning more prominent. Each evening may address more than one facet	Taxing work undertaken well away from competition

40

Running drills

It is now common practice for runners, particularly sprinters, to use a battery of specially designed training exercises in order to drill certain features of the running action which they hope to assimilate.

Such drills may focus on flexion at the knee joint, with the aim of shortening the working lever and thereby speeding recovery of the limb, and through this leg speed. Drills may also focus on power production as the foot strikes the ground, hip placement, body position, arm action, or general aspects of rhythm, all of which are important individual facets of the whole running action.

Each athlete or coach works to his own personal preference and need. Some of the more popular drills follow.

Drills for sprinters

(1) Back kicks or heel flicks
Balance on the balls of the feet. Keep the hips high and pressed forwards. Bring the knees and heels back alternately, folded close to the buttocks. Some believe this drill is more specific if the knee is brought forwards as the heel is folded.

(2) Speed pike drill
An extension of the above drill in which the trunk is inclined forwards and replicates the body position during the acceleration phase of sprinting.

(3) Walking high knees or walking sprint
A deliberate walking execution of the sprinting action emphasising high knee lift with a cocked foot, the supporting leg extended on to tiptoe, the hips placed under the upright torso, and the full range of arm movement.

(4) Running high knees or prancing or 'lifting' drill
Similar to the walking sprint performed at jogging pace. It is important that the drill is executed with high hips, and with the supporting leg permitted to extend right to the end of its function. If performed too quickly, the high hip position will be lost. This fault is often a symptom of abdominal weakness in younger athletes.

(5) Rhythm skips to five or three count
An intermittent version of the second and third drills in which the high knee is activated on every fifth or third step. It improves the runner's ability to isolate certain body actions and thus aids co-ordination.

(6) Pawing or 'skip B' or reach drill
This is essentially a conditioning drill for the hip flexor and abdominal muscles. It is a bounding, exaggerated running action in which the front leg is folded to hip height, then extended forwards as it is brought to the ground. Athletes who are abdominally weak tend to lean backwards when performing this drill.

(7) Skip pawing or skip reach
A rhythmic, gentler version of the fourth drill, performed with a skipping action. It is claimed that this drill grooves the clawing back action of the front leg when it makes contact with the ground, so vital to modern sprinting.

(8) Straight leg running
Another drill which conditions the hip flexor muscles, the muscles involved in folding the leg in the recovery action, and thus in leg speed. Simply run with straight legs, working solely from the hip joint.

(9) Bounding steps or 'Highland fling'
An exaggerated version of the triple jump step phase which is used to develop the leg extensor muscles.

(10) Arm action
First walk the drill, concentrating on driving the elbows backwards while keeping the shoulders low. Run the drill as you become more proficient.

Barrier drills for hurdlers and steeplechasers

It is common practice to refer to special hurdle drills as 'isolation' drills because they isolate particular aspects of the hurdling skill.

(1) Walkovers
This drill corresponds closely to the third sprinting drill. The athlete walks over low hurdles spaced closely enough to force him to lead with alternate legs, or to permit only one small step in between. Emphasis should be placed on keeping the hips high and pressed forwards.

(2) Trail leg drill
The athlete walks or runs down the lead leg side of the hurdles and works the lateral trailing leg action as he passes along them. It is important that the lead foot is placed beyond the barrier, and that the trailing knee is brought ahead of the body to hip height at the mid-line, having crossed the barrier. This drill can be performed with hurdles spaced at intervals demanding one stride, three stride or five stride rhythms.

(3) Lead leg drill
This exercise is performed down the trailing leg side of the hurdles with the lead leg going over the barrier in the normal way, but the trailing leg brought forwards in a pendulous way (i.e. hanging loosely) to the side of the barrier. Once mastered, the speed of pick-up of the lead leg should be accentuated. A high hip presentation is also important. The drills can be performed at three and five stride rhythms.

(4) Alternate hurdle drills
Hurdles are placed alternately in adjacent lanes. This arrangement makes it possible for the athlete to alternate between lead leg and trail leg practices as he runs over the hurdles.

(5) Alternate leg drills
These are useful for 400 metre hurdlers and steeplechasers. The hurdles need to be placed at four stride spacings.

(6) Water-jump practices
Water-jump work can be practised effectively by placing a barrier across the end of the long jump pit and drawing a line across the sand 3.66 m away from it. In this way the laborious process of filling the water trough is avoided, and repeated stress on the landing foot is reduced.

Resistance training

Resistance training offers a further means of creating overload (a loading which is greater than that to which the body is accustomed) against which the body must work. Its most convenient form is in running up hills and it provides a popular form of training for speedster and endurance runner alike. It may take the form of a continuous run in which several hills are traversed, or a repetition session in which each run is made up the same incline. Severity can be adjusted by judicious selection of incline and of the speed at which it is run. Careful selection can also tilt the training's benefits towards cardio-vascular efficiency or towards leg muscle strength.

Sand hills can provide a challenging and more demanding alternative to ordinary hills if they are at hand, and running in surf or in snow also affords mild overload.

Resistances suitable for endurance athletes can be provided by carrying weights strapped to the wrists or ankles, or carried on one's back in a haversack. Care has to be taken to ensure that they are not so heavy as to disturb technique.

Speedsters and short endurance runners frequently tow resistances in their training. Suitable resistances can be provided by the coach or the training partner hanging on to ropes attached to the runner's waist, or by the athlete dragging a weighted sled or worn-out tyre in a similar fashion, or by towing a special parachute. Once again, one must be careful not to disturb technique too greatly.

Another feature of resistance training can be created by using one's own body as the resistance when undertaking conditioning training employing callisthenics such as press-ups, sit-ups, free standing squats, etc.

Medicine balls offer a type of resistance training which develops speed qualities and elastic muscle strength, and are essential to those involved in speed events.

Barbells, dumb-bells, stacked weight sets and isokinetic machines also provide resistance conditioning. They are perhaps most appropriate to the needs of speed athletes, but middle distance athletes should not ignore their value.

Some of the most popular resistance exercises are pictured on pages 43–45, but as the athlete becomes more experienced, there will be a need to seek specialist advice on each of the areas if proper progression is to be made.

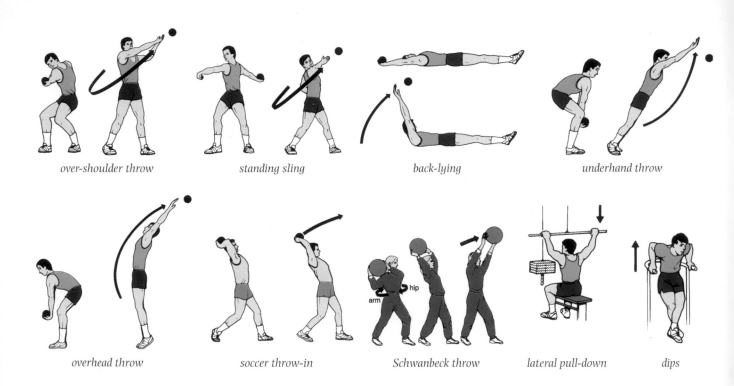

over-shoulder throw   *standing sling*   *back-lying*   *underhand throw*

overhead throw   *soccer throw-in*   *Schwanbeck throw*   *lateral pull-down*   *dips*

▲ *Fig.6 Some training exercises*
(see also page 45)

44

straddle split squat

bench press

leg extensions

back squat

seated press

inclined sit-ups   leg press

spring jumping

depth jumping (for distance)

back dorsal raise

hurdle bounding

depth jumping (for height)

Drugs

The use of drugs by athletes represents a gross violation of the basic ethics of the sport. It is condemned out of hand on two counts.

- It is cheating, and contravenes all principles of fair competition, a concept which represents the core ethos of the sport.
- It represents a social evil by being dangerous to health (some drugs are addictive).

International and national federations now invest considerable finance and energy into developing ever more sophisticated means of detection. Random testing outside the competition season is fast becoming standard practice worldwide. Detected abusers are banned from competition for long periods; in some countries for life.

Lists of banned substances are available from national federations. Ignorance is not accepted as an excuse if you are found to have taken accidentally a banned drug, even if you have done so for perfectly legitimate reasons. Consultation with your doctor on such matters is a sensible precaution.

Competitively, it is not worth even thinking about cheating on such a scale, nor is it worth it ultimately in terms of one's own health. After all, athletics is supposed to be a health promoting activity!

UK Athletics

Athletics House
10 Harborne Road
Edgbaston
Birmingham B15 3AA

Tel: 0121 456 5098
Fax: 0121 456 4998
E-mail: information @ukathletics.org.uk
Website: www.ukathletics.org

International Amateur Athletic Federation

17 rue Princesse Florestine
3P 359
MC 98007
Monaco

Tel: 00 377 9310 8888
Fax: 00 377 9315 9515
E-mail: headquarters @iaaf.org
Website: www.iaaf.org